Plus 2, Minus 2

Ann H. Matzke

www.rourkepublishing.com

www.rourkepublishing.com

PHOTO CREDITS: Cover © Qwasyx; Title Page © Gamutstockimagespvtltd; Page 3 © Sergio Hayashi, Vyacheslav Anyakin, Scrombeen, Inkaphotoimage; Page 4 © Elaromy; Page 5 ©Elaromy, imv; Page 6 © imv; Page 7 ©Elaromy; Page 8, 9 © Olegd, Oleg Shelomentsev; Page 10 © Oleg Shelomentsev; Page 11 © Tyback; Page 12 © Mykola Mazuryk, Vyacheslav Anyakin; Page 13 © Sergio Hayashi, Mykola Mazuryk, Vyacheslav Anyakin; Page 14 © Sergio Hayashi, Mykola Mazuryk; Page 15 © Mykola Mazuryk, Vyacheslav Anyakin; Page 16, 17, 18, 19 © Scrombeen, Inkaphotoimage; Page 20, 21, 22, 23 © Photka, Christasvengel

Written by Luana Mitten

Cover and Interior design by Teri Intzegian

Library of Congress Cataloging-in-Publication Data

Matzke, Ann
Plus 2, Minus 2 / Ann Matzke.
    p. cm. -- (Little World Math)
Includes bibliographical references and index.
ISBN 978-1-61741-762-7 (hard cover) (alk. paper)
ISBN 978-1-61741-964-5 (soft cover)
Library of Congress Control Number: 2011924809

Rourke Publishing
Printed in the United States of America, North Mankato, Minnesota
060711
060711CL

www.rourkepublishing.com - rourke@rourkepublishing.com
Post Office Box 643328 Vero Beach, Florida 32964

Plus two adds two more.

Minus two takes two away.

Let's explore and count along the way.

See three butterflies.

Two more flutter nearby.

3
+2
___

= ?

1

2

Now count the butterflies.

3

4

5

Five butterflies fly.

Four shoes in a row.

Put two shoes away.

$$\begin{array}{r} 4 \\ -2 \\ \hline ? \end{array}$$

1
2

Now count the shoes.

Two shoes dance and play.

One seashell in the sand.

Two more wash ashore.

$$1$$
$$+2$$
$$= \; ?$$

Now count the seashells.

1

2

Three seashells at the seashore.

3

Decorate eight cupcakes.

Give two away.

$$\begin{array}{r} 8 \\ -2 \\ \hline ? \end{array}$$

Now count the cupcakes.

1

2

3

Six fancy cupcakes. Hooray!

4

5

6

Three kites in flight.

Two kites dip out of sight.

$$\begin{array}{r} 3 \\ -2 \\ \hline ? \end{array}$$

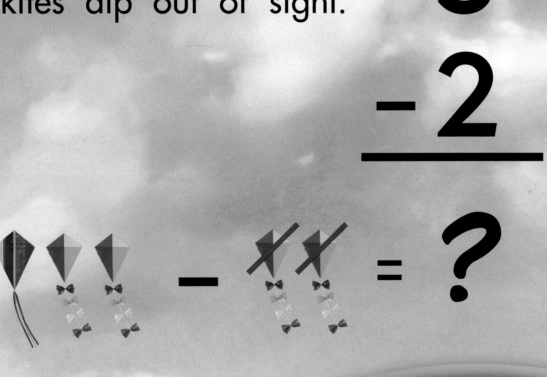

One bright kite, all right!

Adding two or taking away two changes a number by two.

Index

Websites

www.softschools.com/math/addition/learning_addition_for_kids/

www.softschools.com/coloring_games/coloring_umbrellaadd.jsp

www.ixl.com/math/practice/grade-1-adding-2

www.ixl.com/math/practice/grade-1-subtracting-2

About the Author

Ann Matzke is a librarian. She lives with her family in the Wild Horse Valley along the old Mormon Trail in Gothenburg, Nebraska. Ann enjoys reading and writing books.